Surviving a Year

by James Cornette

ISBN-13: 978-1503165229
ISBN-10: 1503165221

1. Rope yourself in
2. Wake to the question
3. NEVER miss a day
4. Build an audience
5. Steal
6. Vampire your life
7. Fake it
8. Mix it up
9. Get uncomfortable
10. Surplus is a must
11. Play some reruns
12. Time travel

It's just 1 photo a day for a year. It sounded easy enough. "It would be fun," I thought to myself. I even convinced a few friends to join the fun. After all, we are designers. "We'll stay fresh! Think of our portfolios!" I preached. And I had to be right...right?

Then came the 4 horsemen of the designer's apocalypse. Stress, Boredom, Laziness, and Fatigue. Within weeks, the stress of the day job and life responsibilities would rear their ugly heads. Months in, I would be battling boredom and laziness. Then, halfway through, I would truly be fatigued and questioning the effort required to finish. I saw friends drop off. I determined to stick to it and I had a few "triggers" that kept me in the game.

Since you're reading this, I assume you've set out on a creative endurance endeavor of your own. Ideas are nothing if they simply sit on the shelf of your mind and aren't fed with action. You're past that. You are a few weeks into what seemed like a great, adventurous idea but have found yourself at the edge of a vast ocean with no wind in your sails. That's OK. You are not alone. I would love to share a few points that helped invigorate my flagging venture.

Let's do this!

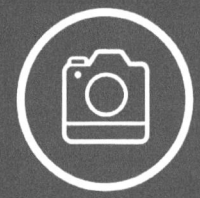

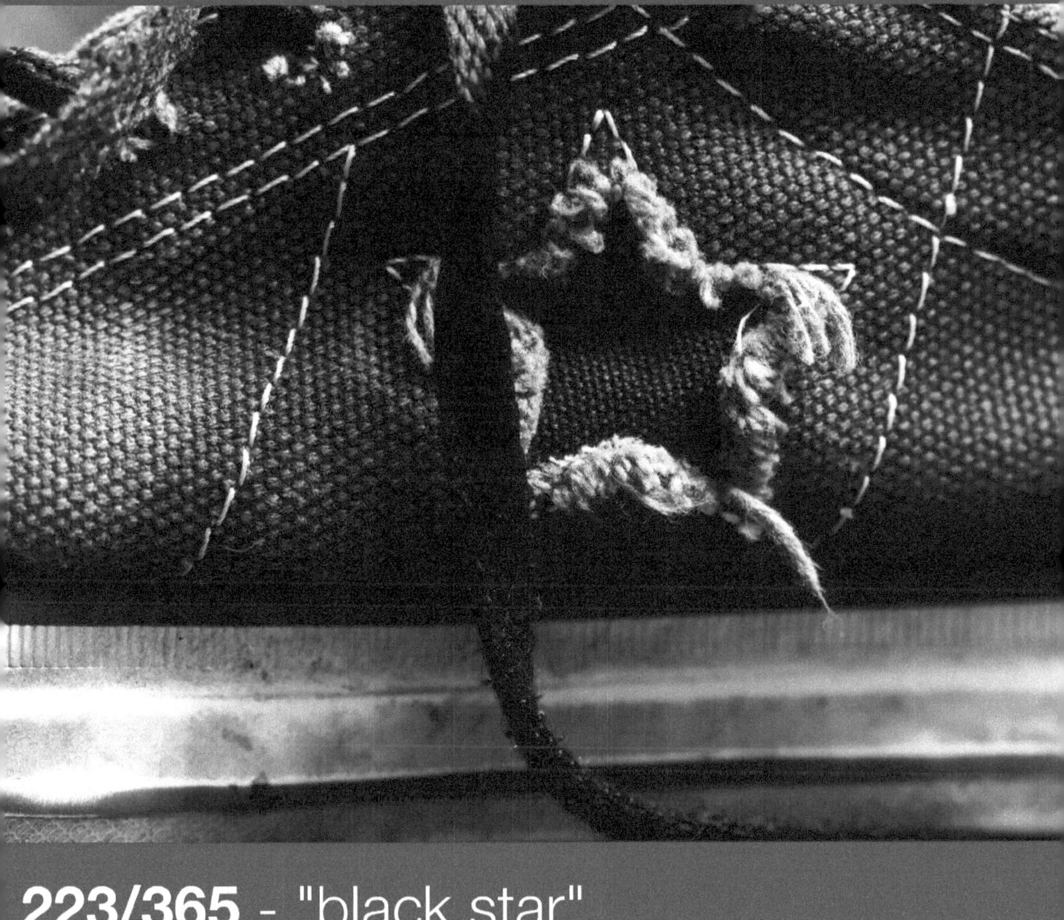

223/365 - "black star"

1. Rope yourself in

Contrary to the naive mind of my youth, I believed that no rules or boundaries equaled unbound creativity. Soon, I found that facing a blank canvas triggered a "deer in the headlights" mind freeze. A blank canvas challenged me with the shrieking siren call of "make something REALLY cool."

If you are anything like me, the open-ended projects are fertile ground for avoidance, mind-wandering, lack of focus, and wasted hours. If your goal is to complete something concrete, you have to lay down some ground rules. Think of the rules as ropes to keep you lightly fenced in. Us creative types like to wander off a lot!

For those critics out there who are borderline anarchists, let me be the first to say that the "rope" of rules can be gnawed through if needed! I have no problem breaking a few rules to complete the goal...but with no rules comes free-form drifting. Trust me on this.

The rules don't need to be complex. They are set up to contain your energy and focus. For the 365 project, the rules were very simple:

1. Post 1 photo EVERY DAY.

2. Each shot must be taken before midnight of that day (Your carriage turns back into a pumpkin at midnight!)

3. No stockpiling photos! This equals laziness later on and kills the growth you will experience shooting daily. If you have trouble picking your photo from several great options, simply open an alternate "B" gallery for the extra shots taken.

With the rules out of the way, I penciled a set of smaller guidelines to help me through. That Sunday evening, my wife was planning out the meals for the coming week as I began mapping out my photos. Monday might be a theme like "Something green," and Tuesday I may draw inspiration from a word. I kept it loose—days could be switched around—but it gave me something to look for and work toward. A simple set of "guidelines" could look like this:

1. Use a theme

2. Choose a word and shoot a photo around that

3. Mimic your favorite influence

4. And the dreaded...let someone ELSE pick for you

The smaller details were left open-ended. You could use photoshop, lightroom, or any tool(s) of your choice to tweak your photographs and you could post to whatever online service you preferred or not at all (this could be a purely personal project, right?). The initial goal is to set some basic rules that you're going to follow and then get photographing.

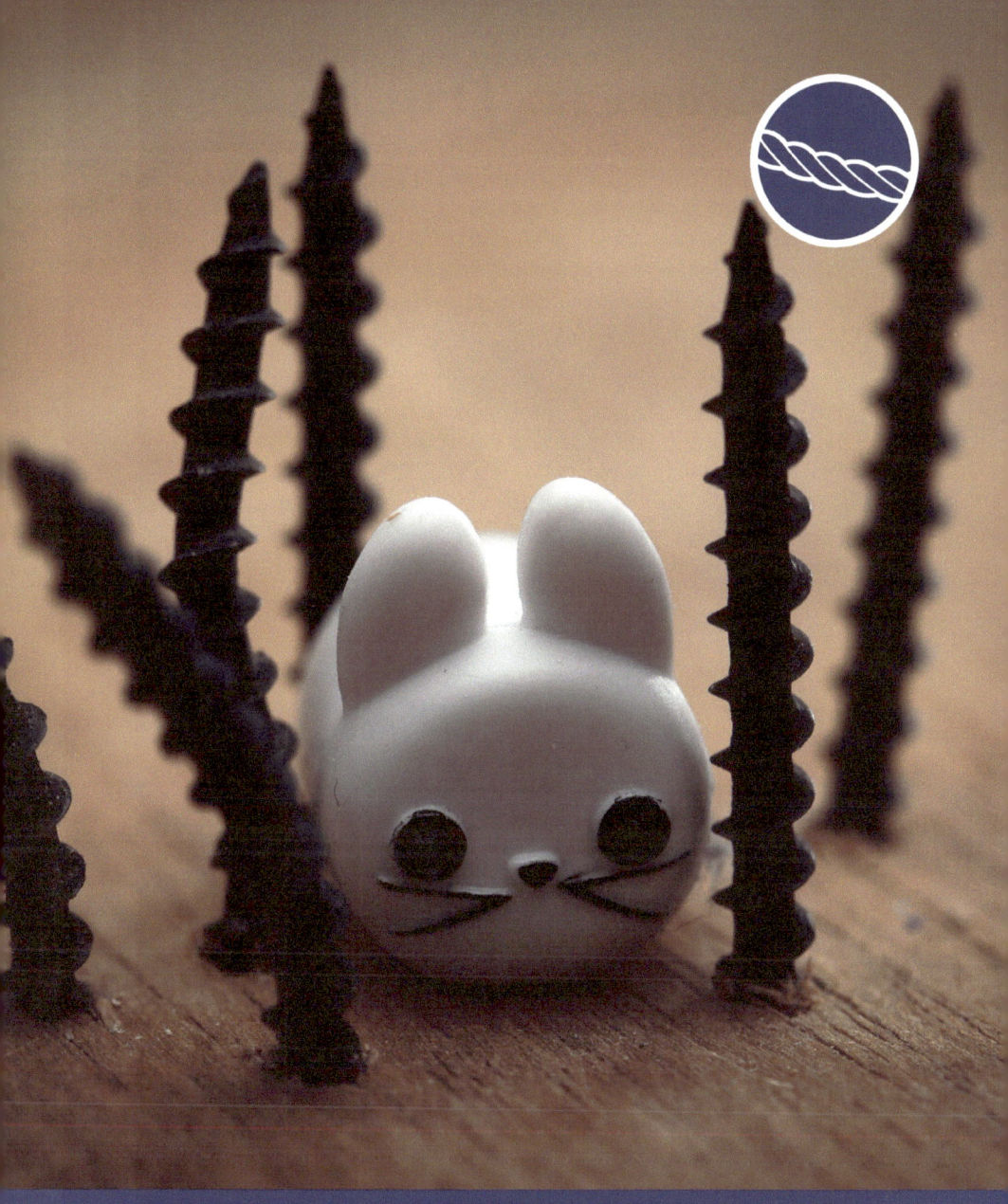

003/365 - "safe"

2. Wake to the question

Let's be honest, it's not a 364 day project (although it would be 366 if you choose a leap year). Miss 1 day early on and you will drop out. I can say this with confidence because I am a victim of this pattern. I miss a few and I am apt to bail. I have watched a few friends do just that. We agreed to start a Tumblr blog called the "Daily Pain" (daily-pain.tumblr.com). We named it such because we knew, at times, it would be a pain.

We started off extremely energized and ready to end the year with a collection of creative work. Then, life got in the way. One by one, participants started dropping off like plague victims. Every day you miss makes the next miss that much easier. They say you never regret a workout, but you always regret skipping one. This is like that, but less sweaty. Here are a few of the inner voices that speak up:

"This is way too much work."

"I will make up for it tomorrow."

"I just don't have time."

"I will just do this next year."

You may get in the middle and feel it is not worth the effort.
That's OK. No one will die if you quit and no one will hate you for it.
BUT, you will definitely miss out on the joy of looking back at a fantastic journey documented for a year. Each photo will trigger fond (and maybe not-so-fond) memories. The collection you create may even end up as a coffee table book.

Could you post twice on one day to make up the loss? Sure. Things happen. Family and the job come first. In my experience, it rarely works out that way though. Shooting every day makes it a habit. Shooting every day makes you choose between lame reality TV or the shot. Shooting every day becomes more critical the longer you are in it. Missing after 320 sequential photographs is painful! Shooting every day makes you a better manager of your own time.

The benefit of sticking to the daily requirement gives you the power to build your audience, and they will come to expect your photographs (more on this later). You can even make a photoshoot a family event by getting your kids, spouse, girlfriend, boyfriend, or talking horse involved in the process. It should be fun and not a chore. You are creating great photographs and memories that you will be glad you labored for.

278/365 - "serene"

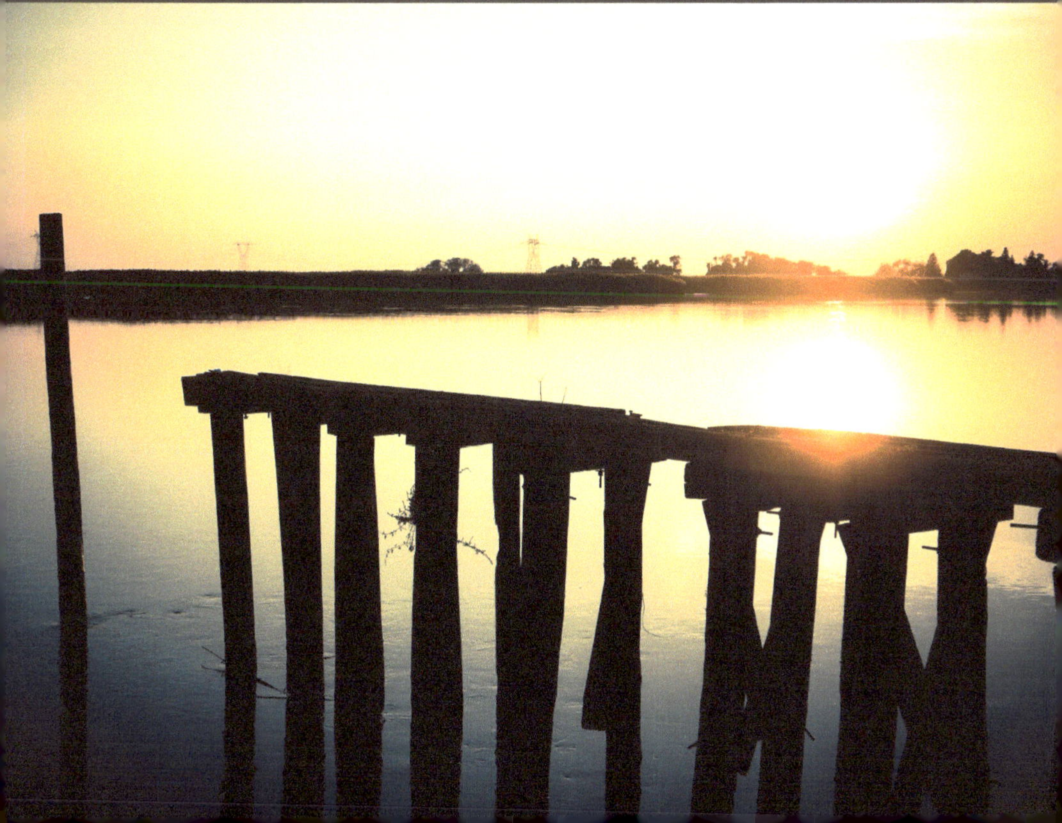

3. NEVER miss a day

Life is noisy. Things get in the way. If I didn't wake up and ask, "What am I going to photograph today?" then, 9 times out of 10, I would struggle near the end of the day on a shot. If I started off (after a cup of coffee) with the right mindset I found myself looking for an opportunity to shoot all day. I would declare something along the lines of, "Today is monotone Monday!", and my loose guidelines would awaken my mind for the day's mission. I would be imagining possible photos on my commute to work or around the office. By making that a part of my day, the opportunities presented themselves.

Ask yourself: "What am I going to photograph today?" The preoccupation with the question makes you less likely to give into your dormant road rage on your morning commute! You are too busy planning a shot to worry about taking "a shot" at the jerk tailgating you in heavy traffic! The question keeps you focused on the goal but also builds up ideas for photos to come. So, pencil down several ideas that can be photographed at a later date, but make sure you pull over onto the shoulder before you start your list. Stockpiling *ideas* doesn't break our rules, but driving and writing simultaneously might.

One word of caution: Don't be *overly* focused on the question. This can get you in trouble with the spouse who is telling you about some important event that day. It can get you flagged in meetings at work for not being "engaged." In a meeting, I've had to ask, "what was the question again?" I missed a question for THE question!

Your mission is set. You now are going to tune into life's details, your curiosities, and opportunities, and you are going to capture them!

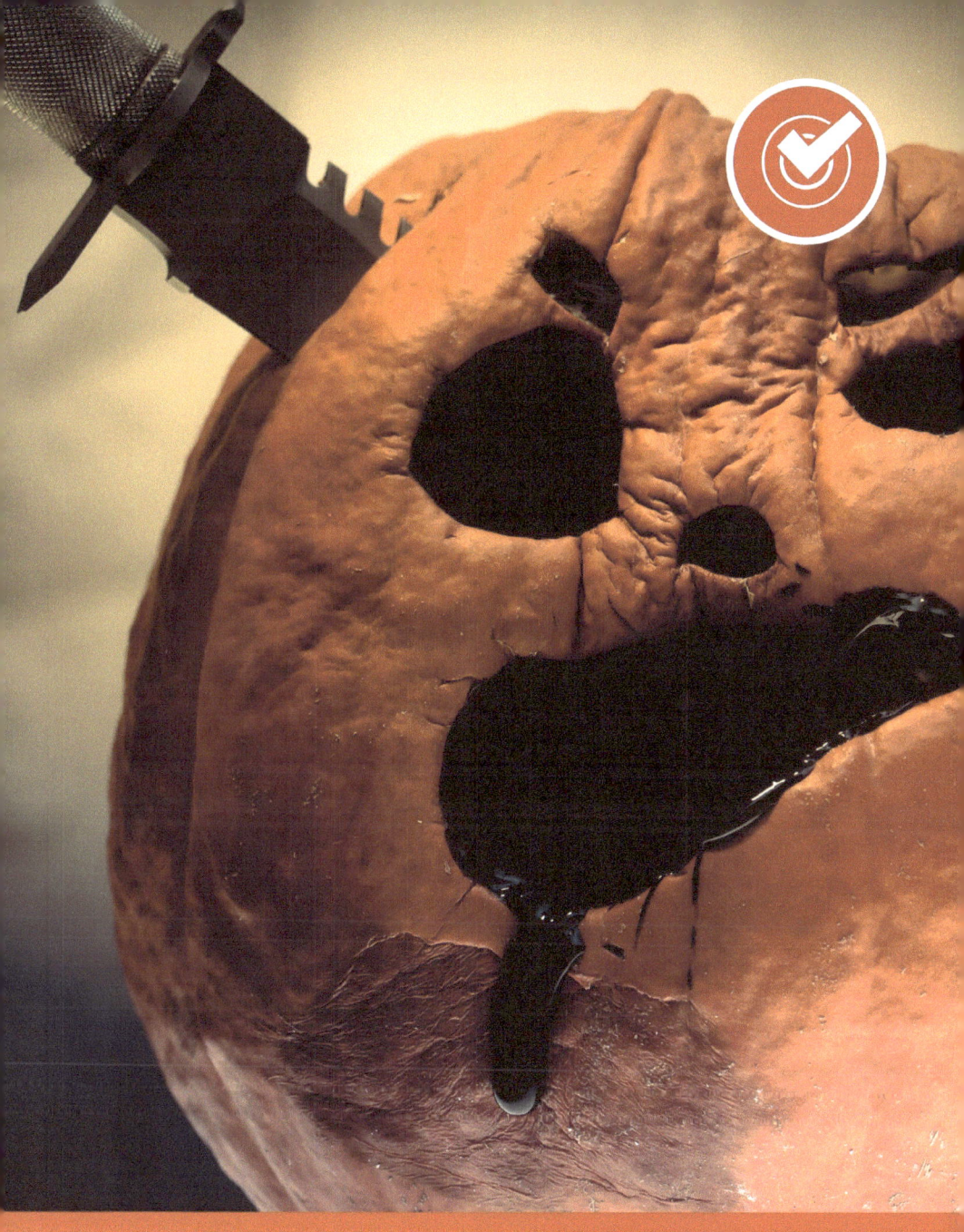

314/365 - "go for the brain"

4. Build an audience

Building a fan base is critical for momentum. You might think an audience is difficult to build, but really only if you're Hannibal Lecter. For the rest of us, the Internet has made this possible with a simple click. Smugmug, Flickr, Tumblr, and Facebook (or whatever your social media preference may be) all have built-in functions to share and be noticed. Thanks to the ability to tag your work, you can join the ranks of searchable content. My fan base started out with Mom, a few siblings, some Facebook friends, and a few unknowns (thanks, Tumblr!). I also posted on Smugmug and have a great community of friends there.

The motivation I feel when receiving a "like" or a comment is fuel in the tank. Having viewers helps "test the waters" for an idea whose success I'm trying to measure. Audience reaction is a great booster when you post a shot that you just weren't digging, yet you get a great response. And, consequently, a group of viewers guilts you in those moments when you are tempted to not post a photo. One of my brothers, who lives several states away, told me once that checking out my "daily" was part of a nightly routine for him and his daughters. He said it was a connection for them to family. That was a powerful statement and has fueled me quite a few times when I was on the edge of bailing.

How does posting to a site generate viewers? For sites like Tumblr, you should use hashtags (#) to label your shot (eg, #365project, #mom, #tommyBirthday). Tumblr users can (and do) search for images via tags. For a photography site like Smugmug, joining a daily community automatically drives your photos to the community photo gallery. Also, using keywords allows your photos to be searched on Smugmug and Flickr. Other means of gaining viewers are to simply post with a clever title and link to your photograph on Twitter or Facebook. Just remember that if you don't tag it, the image can't be indexed or searched on any of the mentioned platforms.

The same way that you make your art visible can be thought of in reverse. You can posse up by seeking out the like-minded. Hashtag and keyword searches (#daily, #dailies, #365, #365photo, etc) in Smugmug, Flickr, Tumblr, and Instagram can reveal fellow 365ers. A little detective work can result in connections with talented, inspiring people.

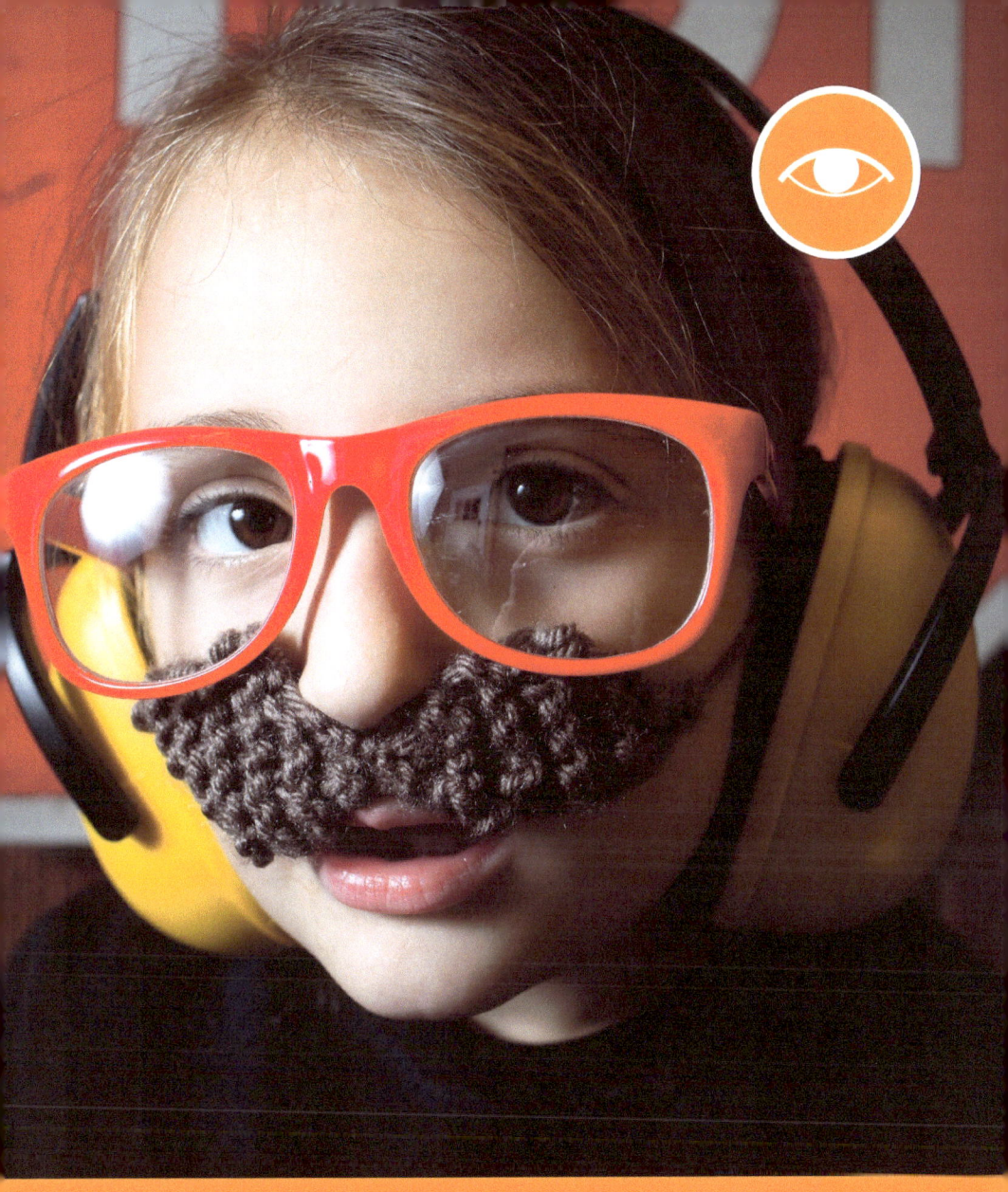

012/365 - "mustacheo"

5. Steal

When I need to learn a new application, the most relevant way for me to learn the tools is to work through a tutorial. I basically mimic someone else's work. The second way is to reverse engineer something I have seen. Yeah, stealing, plagiarism, thievery. I prefer to call it creative borrowing!

Note that, when I stroll down this lane, I give credit where it is due by giving mention and linking to the original photo and creator.

Both of these methods force me to be more cognitive of what I am doing. There are definitely times I will be at a loss for a shot but have a photo in mind that I have seen and LOVE. I will spend time analyzing the composition, lighting, props, and general tone of the image. This can be fun and a great learning opportunity. Experimenting like this helps you better understand lighting and composition.

Morgue File
Keep a collection of inspiring photos on your phone or open a Pinterest account and start an online collection of images you would like to emulate. Such a collection can be a real saver if you are in a creative slump.

"It's not where you take things from,
it's where you take them to.**"**
—Jean-Luc Godard

"Good artists copy, great artists steal.**"**
—Pablo Picasso

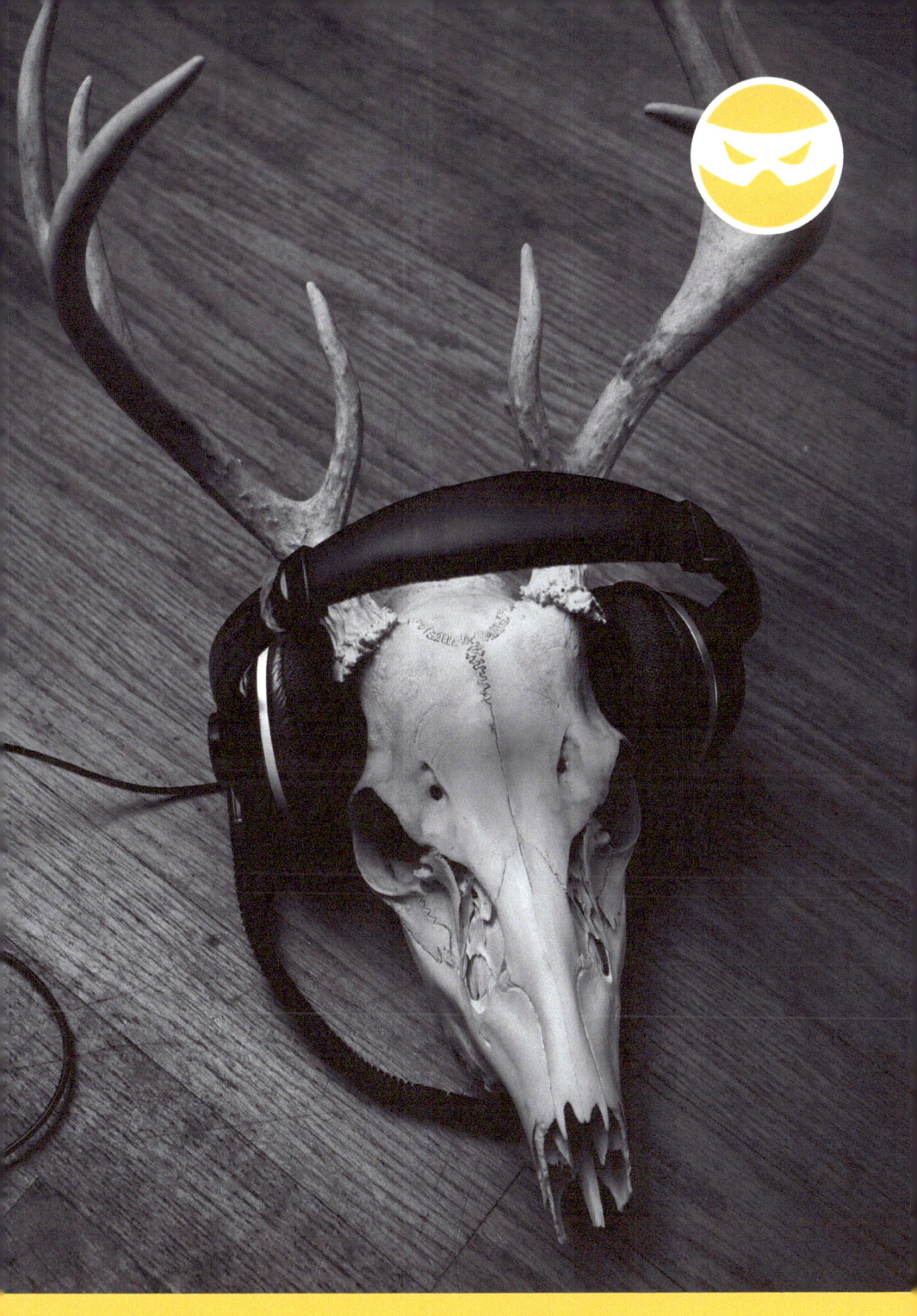

024/365 - "death metal"

6. Vampire your life

Unless you live in a box with zero human contact and never move, every day holds some event worth snagging. It is easy for me to get lost in the daily details of work and family and find myself basically functioning on "auto pilot" without paying attention to a simple life event that would make a great photo. Setting my mind on the daily goal means having my eyes open to the nuances of "the moment." Suck out every drop like a vampire! Remember that those moments will never be exactly the same—each is unique to itself no matter how "simple" it appears. An uncoerced smile or a specific gesture photographed at just the right time is priceless. Moments like these usually have you catching the subject unaware and looking "real". Just avoid going paparazzi on family members! The secret is to ALWAYS have your camera on you and be shooting often. You will soon become background noise and not be noticed! This leaves you free to vampire away (even in the sunlight!).

Be free to share YOUR moments. It is OK to reveal the personal side of your world. This makes you more relatable and keeps you engaged in a year-long journey (your primary goal). Looking back, you will be glad you took the more personal photos as well.

One last thought on this point is that you will be pleasantly surprised to find that the one photo you took that you were unsure about will get a great reaction from some in your audience. So go swoop down on those "common" life moments.

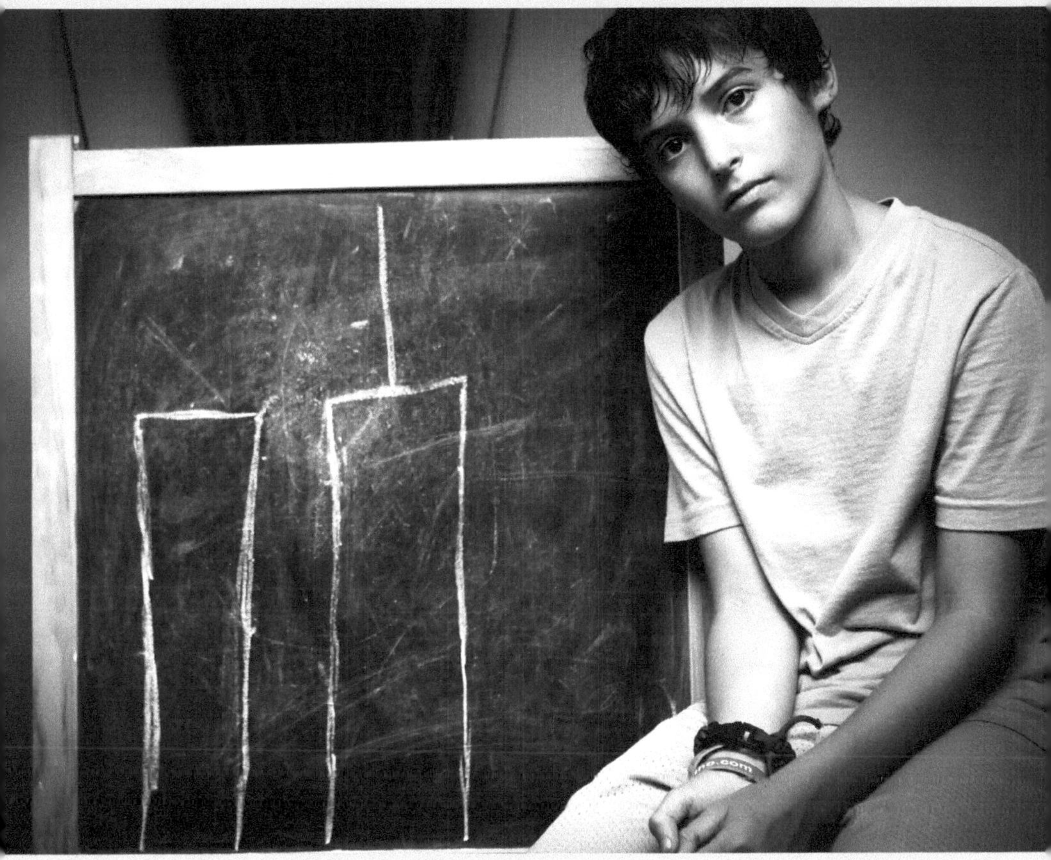

254/365 - "never forget"

7. Fake it

Sometimes a cake needs some more icing. A good photo can become a great shot with the right "addition" to the scene. This point is not for the purists out there. Again, these are points that helped me stay the course and engaged in the project. Altering a photograph can be humorous, creepy, or cinematic. Add a giant godzilla prop to a well-composed city scene or alter the size of a person's head and you have just increased visual interest. I stumbled upon www.onetinyhand.com and was laughing for a solid hour. And, of course, I slipped back to point 5 (steal) and had to mimic a few "tiny hand" shots. It was simply fun and held my interest.

"I don't know photoshop!" is no excuse. There are alternate programs besides photoshop, but the point is simply to stretch your brain and increase your skills. Learning an application opens new options in your work. There are many FREE resources online if you Google "photoshop tutorials." The knowledge comes with the doing.

A great side benefit is to come away with a new technique or acquired skill in a new program. Growth is a plus!

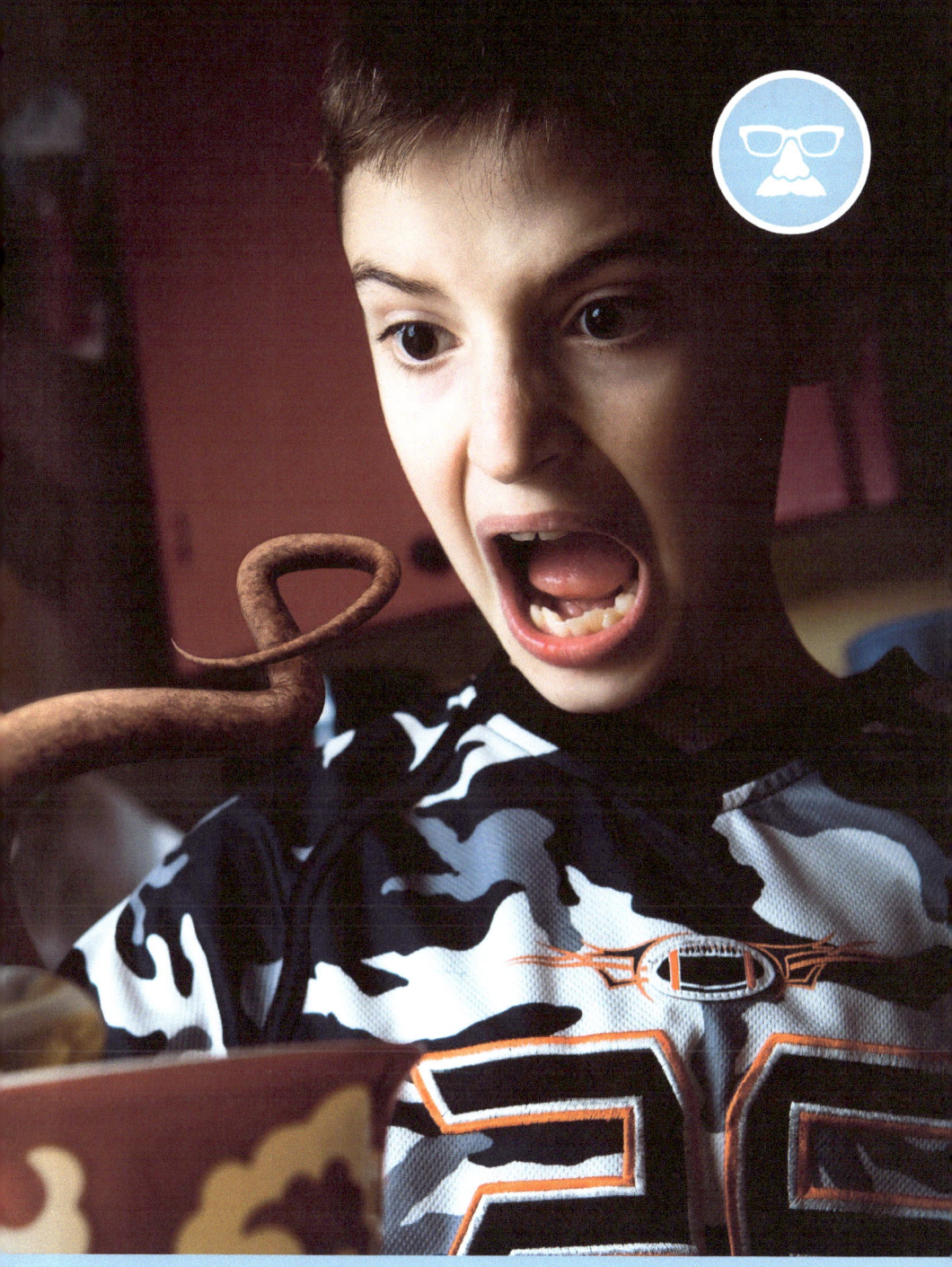

022/365 - "space soup"

8. Mix it up

This is a close cousin to point 7. I am referring to mixing up technique and not necessarily subject matter. Boredom is your enemy. Challenge yourself to learn your camera and add options to your arsenal. You can do a lot with a few "seasonings". Ever shoot with lights or a flash on a budget? Get some cheap shop lights and some white poster board (for bouncing light). Switching the game plan can liven things up. The catch here is that you will need a camera that you can use in manual mode. It also helps to have a few lens options.

Maybe this is even a good time to pick up a book and learn something new about your camera? Try a brand new technique, and let the 365 experiment make you both technically and creatively better. As your knowledge of your tools grows, you will be more free to focus on concept versus technique.

Lighting
EXPERIMENT! The direction and amount of light changes the mood and feel of the image dramatically. There are a few photography sites that actually show you various lighting set-ups and camera settings. A favorite site of mine in regard to off-camea lighting is strobist.blogspot.com. Strobist even has Lighting 101 lessons.

DOF
I shoot shallow depth of field (DOF) a lot! It just looks good. Open aperture equals shallow depth. Also, having an open aperture allows you to shoot with less available light. Good way for me to mix it up and not rely on a "look" is to force myself to close my aperture and shoot with more depth. This makes me consider composition and background items more.

Macro
Going hyper close up creates great textures and opens up new worlds of imagination. Photographing a sheet of paper with a flash aimed across it's surface creates a rough, unique texture. An egg carton looks like the surface of some planet. Get close and discover things your eye doesn't normally pick up.

A few quick points: the more the lens magnifies, the easier it is to get a blurry shot from ANY movement. Tripod up and then shoot. Also, the DOF is VERY shallow, so you will need to close your aperture down to get deeper depth and properly light the scene. And, finally, a macro lens makes a great portrait lens as well.

Cropping
A selective cropping of a shot can mean all the difference in visual interest. Don't be afraid to sacrifice some of the image real estate.

Shoot RAW
Assuming you have a prosumer level camera with the ability to set the data format, always shoot RAW. Shooting in RAW format allows more latitude in post-image adjustments, such as exposure, highlights, shadows, and so on. Basically, you are avoiding any type of image compression (dropped data).

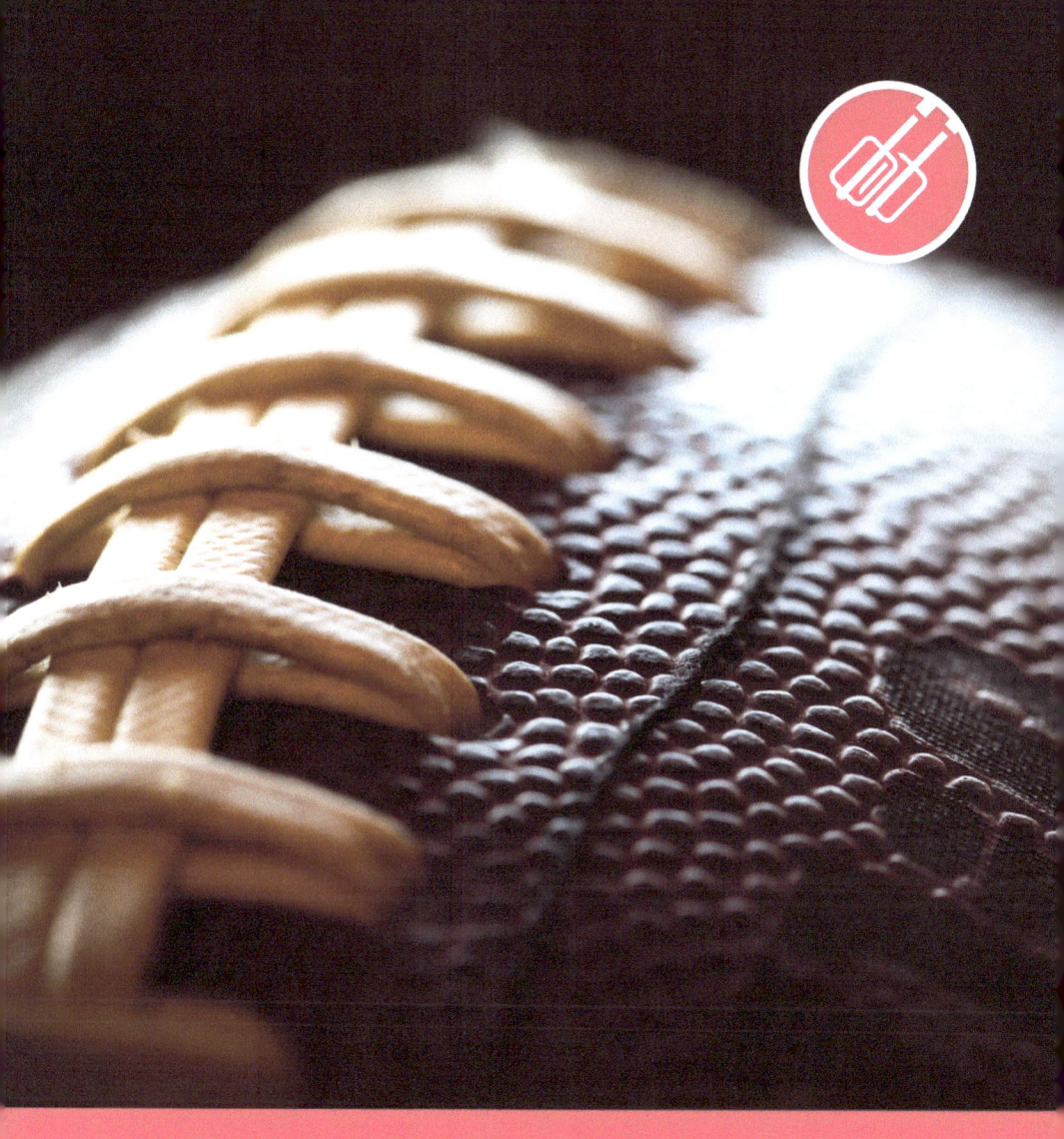

034/365 - "superbowl sunday"

9. Get uncomfortable

Being behind the lens allows me to be a little on the seclusive side. As I am scouring around for location-based shots, I can feel invisible and detached. For me, this is the coward's way out! What do I mean? I will tend to pass up a potential shot of someone to avoid asking if I can take their photo. What if they say no or get angry or ask for money for the shot? These are the strange questions that flood my strange mind! Then I justify not looking for more personal, difficult shots.

Getting "uncomfortable" takes effort and light risk, but it puts me in a place where I can snag a great shot. It also opens up more opportunities and gets me out of a lazy rut.

Being uncomfortable may not necessarily be asking permission of a stranger to take their photo. It may be an uncomfortable situation like a stressful, fast-paced sporting event where you can't exactly set up a shot or a shoot that involves people you have to direct. Whatever your "uncomfortable" is, that is what you tap into to energize your work. You may discover it is a strength you naturally have and enjoy.

One of my "uncomfortables" is to hit the streets of a city to get some close-ups of locals. "How close?" you ask. Close. Philadelphia hosts some great characters. There is never a lack of opportunities. One gentleman in particular screamed out to me...literally! "Hey? You with the news?" he asked. I introduced myself as a hobbyist and offered to buy him a hot cup of joe for his troubles. He agreed and then burst into stories about "Nam" and "UFO probing". I was motivated to take the photo and retreat as quickly as possible!

Note that, for this type of shooting, bigger gear isn't always better gear. Maybe it is a sign of the times (I blame lawyers), but folks tend to be a bit skeptical when you are prowling around with a zoom lens the size of a cannon. I once was questioned by a passing police officer as to "who" I was taking photos of (I blame private eyes) and "why" I was taking pictures of a local theatre. Harmless. Other areas to be careful around are train stations. Yep, detained by police yet again. Be subtle, choose minimal gear, and blend in. Don't ignore your timidness—operate in it.

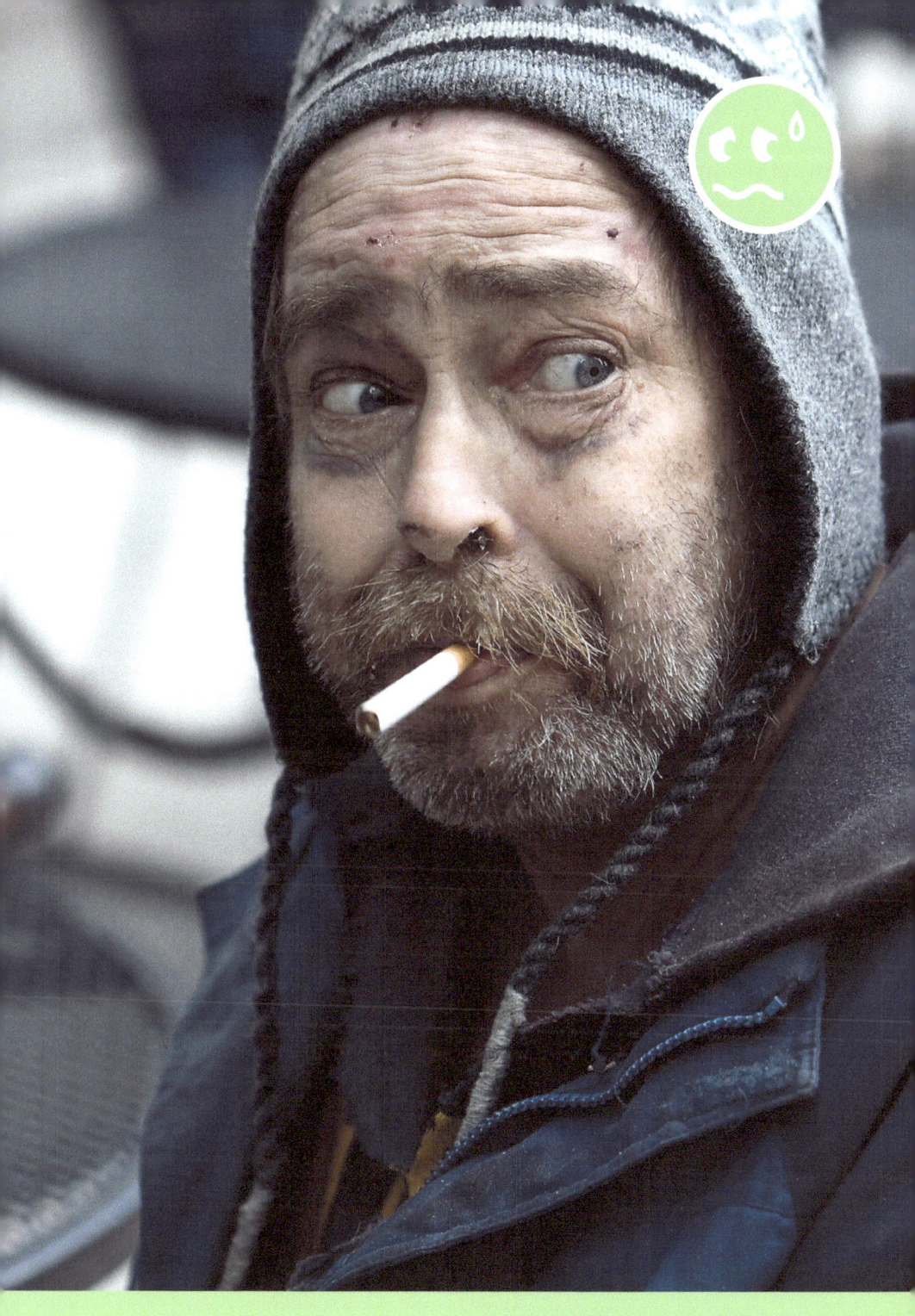

Philly faces - "hey you!"

10. Surplus is a must

Never assume you "got the shot". Many times I had THE shot only to find out that the image was a little soft or had a bad focal point or non-ideal exposure. Shooting extra photos gives you more to work with. This seems obvious, but we all have those over-confident moments or times we shoot just enough to make the cut that day. I would like to point out that if you end the day with less than stellar photos, you still need to post the photo (keeping to point 3). You are not pouring out cash for rolls of film, so shoot away. Have extra memory cards available as well.

What if you have a great day and have multiple images you really like? Making a choice of a single selection is very difficult. I often ask my wife or one of my kids "this one or THIS one?" Mostly, I get a mumbled "uh, I don't know. I like them both I guess." A great solution is to open another gallery and just send the extra photos there. I have a "Misc" gallery and many a homeless photo has landed there. When all else fails, I will just get up, walk away, and come back later with fresh eyes and make a decision then.

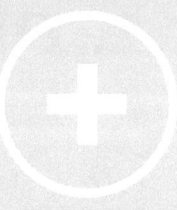

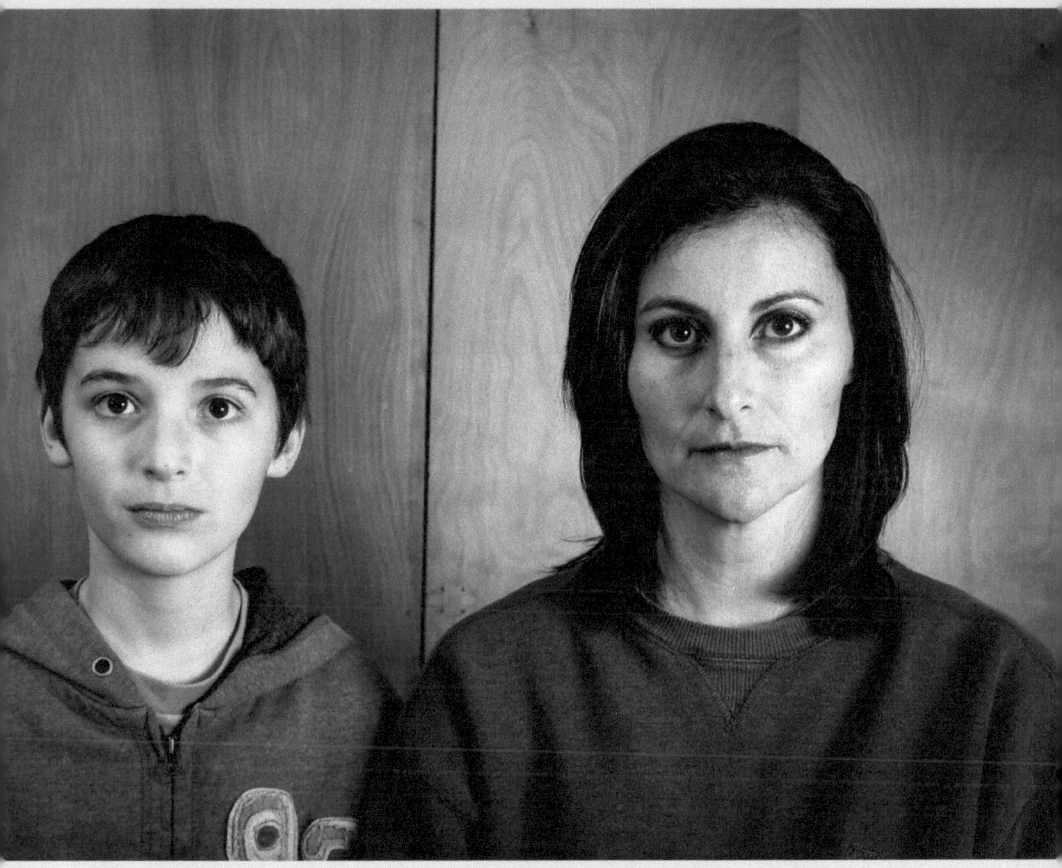

086/365 - "line up"

11. Play some reruns

You can see the light at the end of the tunnel! You have found your stride and have formed creative habits. Then BOOM! Face first into that inevitable wall known as a creative block. Don't panic. It's natural. There were days (more than I care to admit) where my shutter finger was frozen and my motivation was on vacation. I would play a rerun. I would revisit some of my favorite (or failed) photos to date and reshoot one. I could do a variation of the shot. A variation could include:

1. Change the lighting (flash vs no flash, moving/aiming light angle higher or lower to increase drama, time of day)

2. A new angle (photograph a subject from atop a ladder or from a "frog" view)

3. Different depth of field

Keep the variation SIMPLE! Surprise yourself with how a simple reshoot can make a difference! Do a week of reruns where you shoot the same subject at a new angle each day. This would make a great series to hang side by side on a wall. For me, the simple act of freeing myself from the pressure of "what to shoot" and focusing (pun intended) on "how to shoot" energized me.

Another benefit to re-shooting a photo is to see the improvements you've made since beginning this project. Also, you have had time to look at the previous shot and may have had some new inspiration you can now explore. This will also free you up from having to come up with something from scratch. This may be the small "push" you need to keep going.

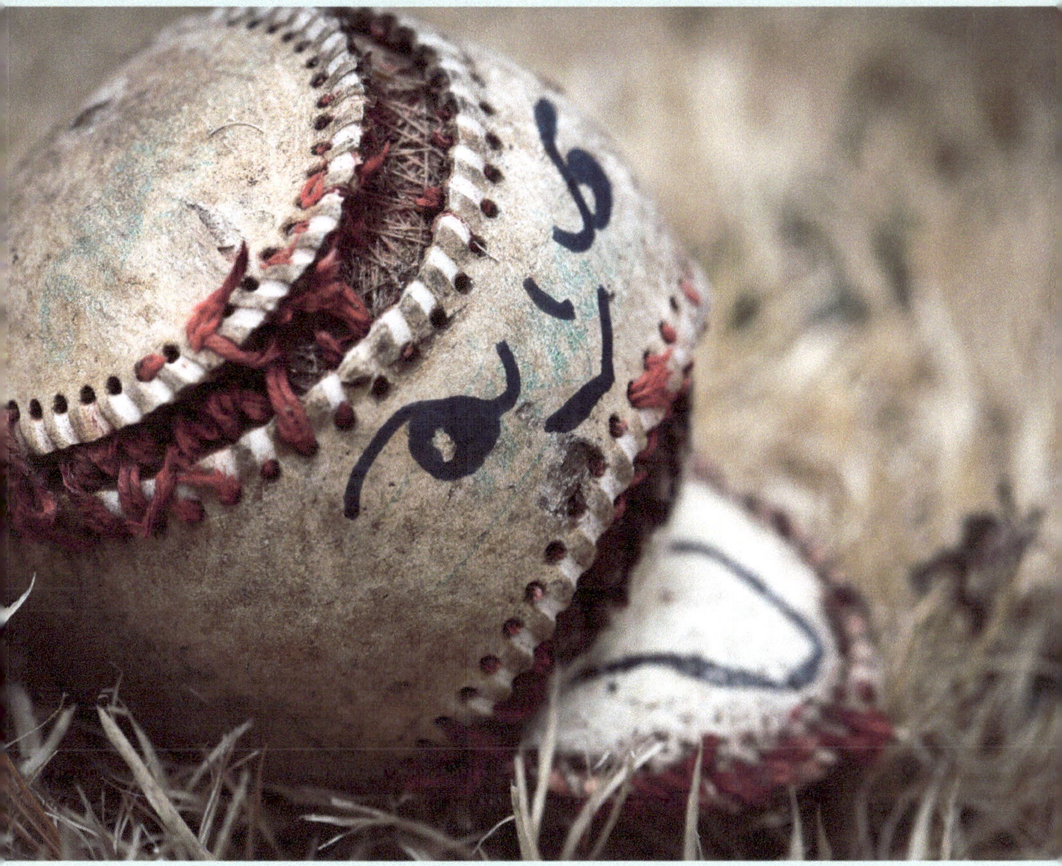

088/365 - "BLAH!"

12. Time travel

Congratulations! You made it 365 days! Now begins your real journey. No camera in hand. Only you and the memories you have captured or created. Travel back to those moments whenever you want. Once-in-a-lifetime smiles, cloud formations, or events that are yours to enjoy and to recount with others. Having all your efforts contained in one location such as Smugmug or Flickr lets you travel in linear fashion to revisit that year in captured clarity. Free time travel without the risk of landing in the middle of a field of angry dinosaurs.

At this point, I recommend that you take a year off and simply enjoy your success. You have earned it! Welcome to the club.

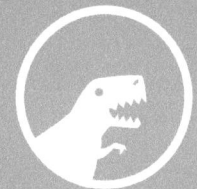

135/365 - "waiting"

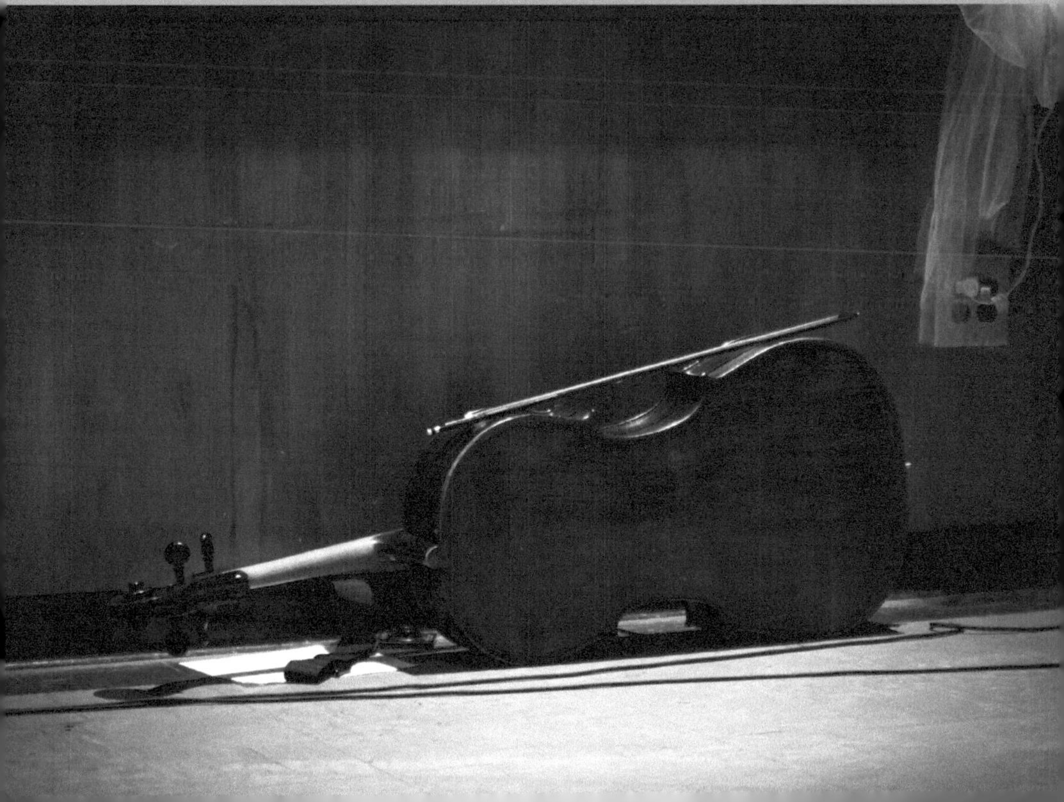

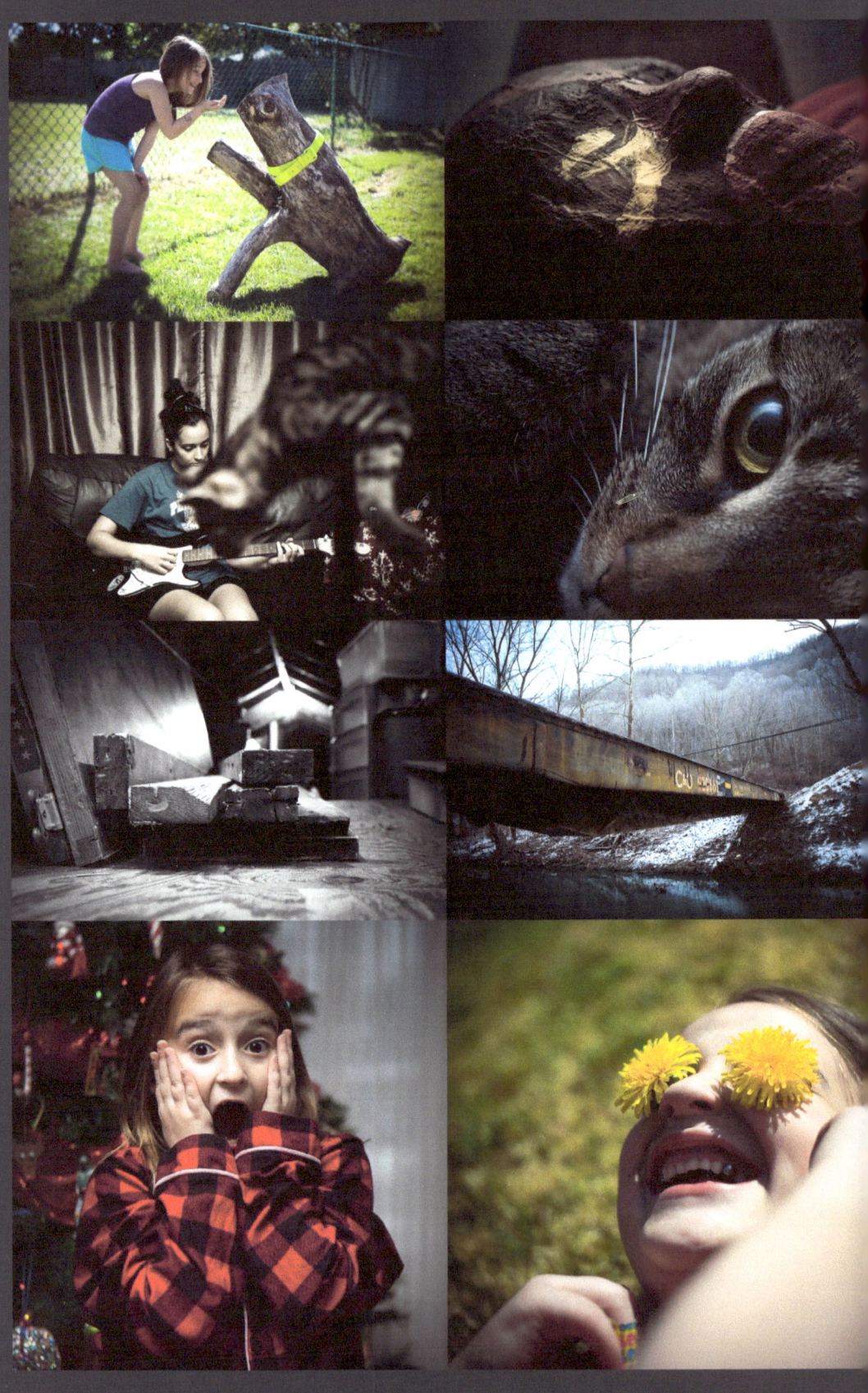

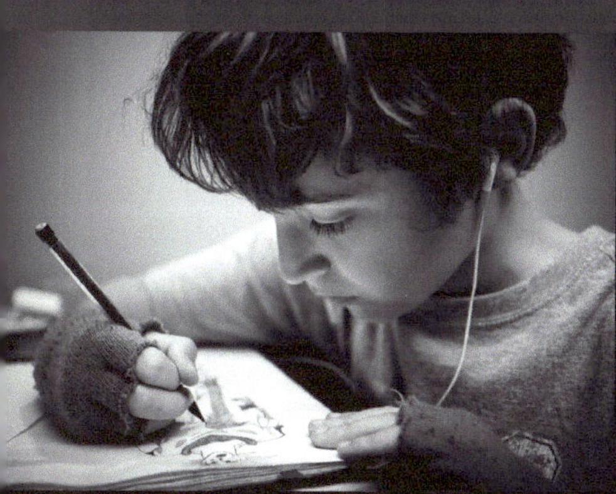

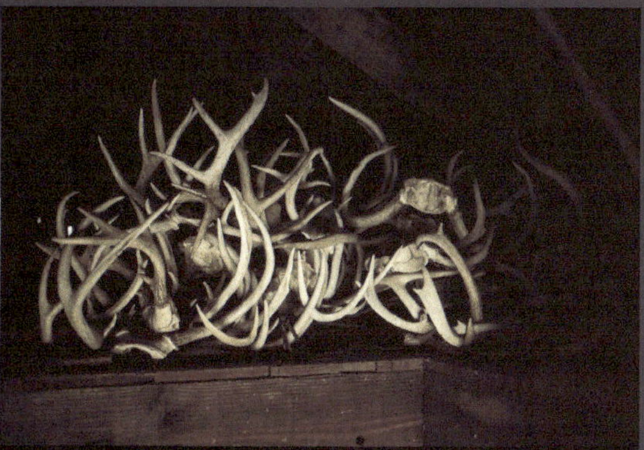

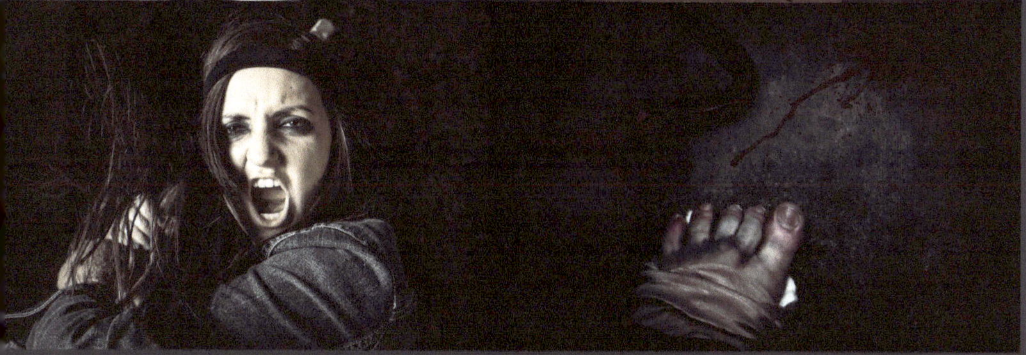

for the complete collection visit:
www.cornfu.com

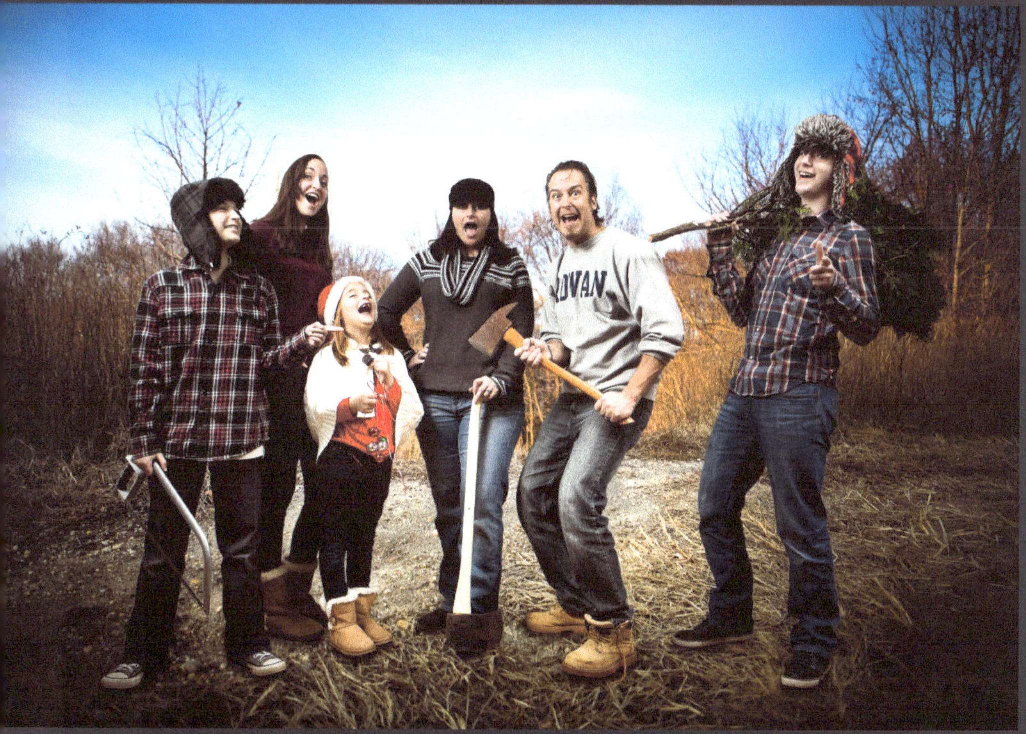

ABOUT THE AUTHOR

James Cornette is an award-winning illustrator and photographer who currently calls southern New Jersey home. He has worked in a range of fields including a car factory, a paint ball distributor, and as an art director at a large pharmaceutical ad agency near Princeton. In his downtime, he loves sketching with his 4 children, spending time behind his camera, and racking up miles on his road bike.

James' photography galleries can be see at www.cornfu.com. His portfolio site is www.jamescornette.com. James' daily sketch project can be viewed at corngrain.tumblr.com

www.cornfu.com
www.jamescornette.com
corngrain.tumblr.com

www.ingramcontent.com/pod-product-compliance
Lightning Source LLC
Chambersburg PA
CBHW041613180526
45159CB00002BC/828